100 Easy Camping Recipes

Bonnie Scott

Table of Contents

100 Easy Camping Recipes

Preparing quick meals on camping trips is easy if you have the right recipes and ingredients. Just wait until you get any of the 100 recipes in this cookbook cooking over an open flame. Camp cooking has never been easier or tastier.

Hot dogs and canned foods are by no means the extent of foods you can prepare easily while camping. If you can cook it at home, you can cook it over a campfire if you bring the needed ingredients and cooking equipment.

Get a head start on any of these recipes by combining the seasonings at home in advance. Store each set in a separate plastic bag, label it and add a copy of the recipe. Cooking out will be a breeze when you are organized and that will leave extra time for fun in the sun.

There are many ways to cook while camping, from grilling to aluminum foil packets to Dutch ovens. Just pop your meat and veggie in aluminum foil, cook it over the campfire and you have a quick and delicious meal. You will find many recipes you'll love inside this camp cooking guide.

Top Tips for Camping with Kids

Camping with the kids is a great way to spend a vacation that's economical and educational. Preparation is the key to a relaxing trip everyone will enjoy.

Rehearsal Campout

If camping is a new experience, a backyard camp-out is a good way to introduce your child to things he may find startling or worrisome. Camping in the backyard gets him accustomed to the spooky night sounds and prepares him for the new things he'll be experiencing.

You can also use this trial run to make notes of things to bring or conveniently forget.

Plan the Trip as a Family

Let the kids help with the planning. Include their food requests, let them pick out toys, games and plan some of the activities. As much as their age and maturity allows, let them be responsible for their own things.

Make the Most of Your Outdoor Adventure

Water, dirt, bugs and other icky stuff are all part of the fun for kids. Let them get filthy, collect disgusting objects and eat things you would cringe at under normal circumstances. Encourage them to explore their surroundings, teaching them safety rules along the way. An outdoor pocket guide of indigenous plants, animals and insects is useful to answer all their questions, and a child-size shovel, bucket and zippered plastic bags to hold their treasures will certainly come in handy.

Bring the Right Equipment and Supplies

You are roughing it, so don't plan to have every modern convenience. Make sure to bring a first aid kit for the inevitable scrapes and bug bites. Bring plenty of sunscreen and a brimmed hat for everyone.

Long pants and long sleeve shirts are sometimes overlooked in the summer, but are helpful for overexposure to sun or cool evenings.

Create Memories

Provide everyone with containers for treasures. Zippered storage bags or lidded plastic containers are inexpensive options.

Provide disposable cameras for each child, or have them take turns with a digital camera to capture impressions of their adventures. Back at home, they can use their photos and collections to create a shadow box or a scrapbook to display their treasures.

Plan for the Unexpected

If the weather turns wet, provide indoor activities to pass the time. Card games, books and other quiet activities can help repel frayed nerves.

Tourist attractions, a trip to a store for supplies or an ice cream parlor can relieve a rainy afternoon of boredom. Although you shouldn't load the car with an entire toy box, younger children will want a few toys. A few toys from the dollar store should be all that is needed.

Camping with kids can be a memorable vacation for everyone. Don't expect perfection and be ready with alternatives. Get away from your schedules and commitments, and focus on your family. The benefits will last long after the sunburn and bug bites have faded away.

Camp Kitchen Basics

Camp cooking can be fun if you are creative, plan ahead and keep things simple. The trick is finding a balance between easy preparation, nutritious ingredients, availability and storage.

Pack the essential equipment, including storage containers, kitchen tools and food supplies. If you've forgotten something, learn to improvise. It's all part of the fun of camping.

Constructing Your Kitchen Area

Set up a sheltered area with a large tarp in case of rain. Position it out of the wind and away from the tents. If you have a campfire, place your kitchen away from the area for safety.

Camp Kitchen Essentials

Water is essential. If you have fresh water available, bring jugs to carry it from the public facilities. If you bring your own water, plan on two to four quarts per person daily. That does not include water for cooking and cleaning.

Stove, fuel and waterproof matches are a must unless you plan to cook all meals over an open campfire.

You'll need a table or a stable flat surface for cooking and food preparation. A folding table is ideal and doesn't take up much space in your car.

A frying pan and a Dutch oven is enough for cooking the simple meals you'll be preparing. Cast iron is best for this type of cooking. A coffee pot can be used to heat water for hot beverages and washing dishes. Don't forget a plastic basin or bowl for dishwashing and clean up, as well as cleaning towels, scrubbies and biodegradable soap.

Along with appropriate dinnerware, bring a sharp knife and cutting board, can opener, large spoon, fork and spatula. Bring plenty of aluminum foil, zippered storage bags and lidded plastic containers.

Bring two coolers. One cooler is used for beverages, as it will be opened frequently. The second cooler is for food items. Freeze as much of the food for this cooler as possible. Open it only when necessary and the contents should remain cold for up to two days.

Learning to make do with what you have is part of the fun and adventure of camping. Just make a list of things you'll need to remember next time, and hone your skills in campground cooking.

Staples to Bring Camping

Don't empty your cupboards for your camping trip. Food and its preparation should be simple using as few ingredients and utensils as possible. Planning your camp kitchen supplies will make cooking easy and minimize cleanup.

Disposable, No Clean Up Cooking

Bring plenty of heavy duty aluminum foil. Use it to line pans for easy clean up. Many recipes use individual foil cooking packets for a meal with virtually no clean up. Shish kabob sticks are useful for cooking meats, vegetables and various other non-kitchen related ideas the kids will invent.

Oils and Spices

Cooking spray is a blessing. It takes up little space, prevents sticking and has no calories. There are sprays for both pans and grills. Bring oil in a sealed, plastic container. Butter or margarine in a plastic tub travels well.

Don't bring your entire spice rack. Choose flavors the family likes. Salt, pepper, garlic and onion powders, seasoned salt and basil are very basic. Add favorites for grilling meats or seasoning stews and casseroles.

Cans and Condiments

Be sure to include your favorite condiments. Ketchup, mustard, Worcestershire, barbeque and teriyaki sauces are all family favorites. Brown sugar is used in a number of main course dishes and desserts.

Salad dressings, dry onion soup mix and salsa are versatile flavorings, and vinegar is useful in cooking and cleaning. Tomato sauce, diced tomatoes and creamed soups are staples that make stews, soups and casseroles easy to prepare quickly.

Canned baked beans and green beans are the start to a number of easy side and main dishes, so be sure to pack a few of your favorite varieties.

Dairy Products
Eggs and cheeses are staples in a campside kitchen. They store well and are versatile for every meal.

Breads, Pasta and Rice
Bisquick® is used for many recipes; fluffy pancakes, hearty dumplings and toppings for cobbler style desserts.
Refrigerator biscuits are useful, if you have proper cold storage.
Tortillas, bread and buns are a mainstay. Use the bread and rolls early in the expedition, and save the tortillas for later use as they have a longer shelf life.
Uncle Ben's® Ready Rice® is great to have on hand for casseroles and to serve as a side for many hearty meals.

Vegetables
Onions, potatoes and carrots keep well. Celery, if kept in an airtight container, will be a welcome addition for flavoring many casseroles and foil pouch meals.

Meats
Hamburger, hotdogs, bacon, chicken breasts and sausage of all kinds are campground staples. Plan your menus around a few basic meat choices. There are so many recipes from which to choose, dinner will never be boring.

Take time to plan quick and easy menus, but don't be rigid. Camping should be fun and relaxing for everyone, including the cook. You will find a printable checklist that will keep your camping organized on our website
www.CampingFreebies.com.

BREAKFAST

Campfire Eggs

1 dozen eggs
1 lb. of bacon (cut into bite size)
1/2 cup onion, chopped
1/2 cup bell pepper, chopped
1 can mushrooms, 4 oz., chopped
Shredded cheddar or pepper jack cheese, 8 oz.

In a cast-iron skillet, fry the cut up bacon until almost done. Add onion, mushrooms and bell pepper and stir until bacon is crisp and vegetables are tender. Crack all 12 eggs into a large bowl and beat well (add a dash of milk if desired). Pour eggs into skillet and stir mixture until eggs are cooked. Sprinkle cheese on top.

Camp French Toast

4 slices of bread
2 eggs
1/2 teaspoon cinnamon
Maple syrup

Non-stick cooking spray

Combine egg and cinnamon in a bowl and submerge the bread in the mix. Spray a frying pan with non-stick cooking spray. Cook the bread in the frying pan over coals or grill to a golden brown. Top with maple syrup.

CAMP MORE ... WORK LESS

Breakfast Burritos

1 ground sausage roll
4 or 5 potatoes
12 eggs
Package of flour tortillas
Shredded American cheese, 8 oz.
Jar of salsa, 16 oz.
Salt and pepper to taste
Pam® cooking spray

Potatoes - Wash, peel and cut potatoes into small cubes.
Spray Pam® in a skillet. Cook the potatoes in the skillet until
they are almost done. Add the sausage and cook until brown.
Add the eggs, salt and pepper. Stir and cook the mixture until
the meat is completely cooked. Serve on flour tortillas and add
salsa and cheese.

Eggs on a Grill

12 eggs
Muffin pan
Pam® cooking spray

Spray the muffin pan with Pam®. Preheat the grill to medium high heat. Crack an egg into each hole of the muffin pan. Place pan on grill and cook for 2 minutes, or until done.

ROUGHING IT

Easy Pancakes

2 cups Bisquick®
1 cup milk
2 eggs
Optional: 1/2 cup strawberries or blueberries

Stir all ingredients until blended. Use 1/4 cup of batter for each pancake.

Pour 1/4 cup batter onto a greased, heated griddle. Cook a couple minutes until bubbles begin to form on top, then turn and cook second side to a golden brown color, another couple minutes. Yield: 14 pancakes.

Omelet in a Baggy

2 eggs per omelet
Cheddar cheese
Large Ziploc® freezer bag

Suggested additions of your choice: chopped tomato, chopped onions, black olives, sliced mushrooms, precooked microwave bacon

Crack the eggs into a large zip-lock freezer bag. Squeeze the air out of the bag and seal it. Squeeze or shake the bag to beat the eggs. Add the rest of the ingredients to the bag. Squeeze out most of the air again and seal the bag. Boil water in a large pot. Place the bag into the boiling water and cook for 13 minutes. Open the bag and the omelet should roll out easily onto a plate.

BEEF

Hobo Dinners

1 lb. hamburger
1 onion, sliced
4 medium potatoes, cubed
1 can of corn (or package of frozen corn)
Salt and pepper to taste
Heavy duty aluminum foil - 4 pieces 18" x 24"

Spray foil with non-stick cooking spray. Put the pieces of foil on a flat surface. Crumble 1/4 of the hamburger in the center of each foil. (This recipe also works if you want to brown the hamburger first in a pan, drain, then add it to the foil.)

Add the sliced onions on top of the hamburger. Salt and pepper the hamburger. And corn on top, then the cubed potatoes. Fold the sides of the foil up as if making a tent. Take the top edges and fold them over together. Then on each end, bring together and fold the edges over together. Be sure the foil is sealed tightly. It will cook faster if it is air tight. Cook over coals 20 to 30 minutes depending on the coals.

Yield: 4 servings.

Meatball Goulash

1 pound hamburger
1 egg, beaten
1/2 cup bread crumbs
1 can tomato sauce, 15 oz.
2 tablespoons olive oil
1/2 teaspoon pepper
1/2 teaspoon oregano
1/4 teaspoon basil
1/2 teaspoon garlic powder
1/4 teaspoon onion powder

Mix the hamburger, egg and bread crumbs. Form the hamburger into small meatballs. Heat the olive oil and brown the meatballs. Add the rest of the ingredients and cook for 15 minutes or until hot. Serve with hot noodles.

Quick Chili

1 pound hamburger
1 onion, chopped or onion flakes
1 can Ranch style beans
1 qt. stewed tomatoes
1 can tomato soup, 10.75 oz.
Salt and pepper to taste
1 teaspoon chili powder

Brown the onion and hamburger together. Drain the fat and add the rest of the ingredients. Cook on medium heat, covered, for 15 to 20 minutes.

Pizzaburgers

1 1/2 pounds hamburger
1 medium onion, chopped
1 can tomato sauce, 8 oz.
1/2 pound shredded mozzarella cheese
6 to 8 chopped olives
Hamburger buns
1/2 teaspoon garlic powder
Oregano
Salt and pepper

Brown the hamburger and onion. Drain. Let cool. When cool, mix in tomato sauce and spices. Add the mozzarella cheese and chopped olives. Spoon on hamburger buns. Sprinkle lightly with oregano.

Wrap each bun separately in aluminum foil. Seal foil, checking for leaks. Place on hot coals for 10 to 15 minutes per side. (or cook in 350 degree F oven for 20 minutes in foil.)

Roast with Vegetables

3 to 4 pound chuck roast
2 potatoes
2 ears of corn
Spices to season

Season a chuck roast and wrap in heavy duty aluminum foil. Place on a trivet in a Dutch oven. Cover and cook on a medium fire grill for 45 minutes. Wrap the corn and potatoes separately in aluminum foil and cook for 3 hours over a very low flame.

Quick Stroganoff

1 pound hamburger
1 medium onion, chopped
1 can cream of mushroom soup, 10.5 oz.
1 can cream of chicken soup, 10.5 oz.
1/2 pint sour cream

Brown hamburger and onion. Salt and pepper to taste. Drain grease. Add both cans of soup with only 1 can of water. Simmer for 20 minutes. Add the sour cream and heat through just before serving. Serve over rice or toast.

Cola Hamburgers

1 to 1 1/2 lbs. ground beef
1/4 cup Coca-Cola®
1/2 cup saltine crackers, crushed
1 egg
2 tablespoons ketchup or French dressing
2 teaspoons Parmesan cheese, grated
Pam® grilling spray
Hamburger buns

Preheat grill to medium-high heat. Spray the grill with Pam®. In a bowl, mix the crackers, ketchup or dressing, cheese and the cola. Mix in the ground beef. Form into 6 patties. Grill for 15 to 20 minutes, until done.

Steak Hobo Dinners

2 to 3 steaks
1 onion, sliced
2 potatoes
8 tablespoons margarine
Salt and pepper
Heavy duty aluminum foil – 4 pieces 18" x 24"
Non-stick cooking spray

Wash the potatoes and leave the skin on. Cut potatoes into 1" cubes. Cut the steaks into 1" pieces. Spray foil with non-stick cooking spray.

Add a tablespoon of margarine in the center of each piece of foil. Put the potatoes on top of the butter on all 4 pieces of foil. Layer the sliced onions on top of the potatoes. Layer the steak pieces on top of the onions. Add salt and pepper. Put another teaspoon of margarine on top of the steak.

Gather up the sides of the foil and seal into little packets. Leave room in the packet for heat expansion. Grill over medium high heat for 35 to 45 minutes.

Campground Hotdish

1 lb. hamburger
1/2 green pepper, chopped
1 onion, chopped
1 can tomato sauce, 15 oz.
1/2 teaspoon Worcestershire sauce

Brown hamburger, onion and green pepper. Drain grease, add tomato sauce and Worcestershire sauce. Cook 1/2 hour longer.

 WE'RE SLEEPING WHERE?

Hamburger Patties in Foil

Hamburger (1 patty per person)
Potatoes, each cut in 8 pieces
Chopped onion
Chopped celery
Salt & pepper to taste
Heavy duty aluminum foil – one per person 18" x 24"

Place all the ingredients on a square of heavy duty aluminum foil and wrap tightly. Place on hot coals or grill. Cook for 15 minutes, then turn and cook for another 15 minutes or until meat is cooked and potatoes are tender.

Campfire Stew

1 8 oz. roast
1 potato
2 carrots
1 onion
1 can of corn, 14.75 oz., drained
1 tablespoon butter
Salt and pepper
Heavy duty aluminum foil – 18" x 24"

Cut the potato into 1/2" squares. Slice the carrots and onion. Cut the roast into 1" pieces. Spray the foil with non-stick cooking spray, then layer the roast, potatoes, corn, onion and carrots. Add salt and pepper, butter and a tablespoon of water on top.

Fold edges of the foil together; seal the ends. Set the foil packet in coals or grill for an hour.

Bean and Hamburger Casserole

1 lb. ground beef
1 small onion, chopped
2 cans baked beans, 15 oz. cans
1/2 cup barbecue sauce
Package of fully cooked bacon
1 cup shredded cheddar cheese
Refrigerated biscuit dough
Salt and pepper to taste

Cook the hamburger and onion in a large skillet or Dutch oven over medium heat until onion is tender and hamburger is done. Add salt and pepper and drain.

Break the bacon into small pieces. Add the bacon bits, beans and barbecue sauce to the ground beef and bring to a boil. Lower the heat to medium low. Arrange the biscuits side by side over the top of the hamburger mixture.

Cover and simmer for about 10 minutes or until the biscuits are done. Sprinkle cheddar cheese on top. Put a biscuit on each plate and spoon the mixture over the biscuits.

Barbecued Beef Ribs

3 lbs. beef short ribs with bone
1 tablespoon vegetable oil
1 can tomato paste, 6 oz.
1 cup ketchup
3/4 cup brown sugar
1/2 cup chopped onion
1/2 cup vinegar
2 tablespoons prepared mustard
Salt to taste

In a Dutch oven over medium-hot heat, brown the ribs in the vegetable oil. Add 2 cups of water and bring to a boil. Cover Dutch oven and simmer for 1 1/2 hours. Drain the water. Combine the rest of the ingredients with 1/2 cup of water. Pour over ribs. Return to heat, cover and simmer for 1 hour until meat is tender, stirring occasionally.

Camp Roast

1 chuck roast - 3 to 4 lbs.
2 cups barbecue sauce
3 potatoes
4 carrots
1 onion
Heavy duty aluminum foil – 18" x 24"

Peel and slice the potatoes, onion and carrots. On a piece of aluminum foil, pour 1 cup of the barbecue sauce. Put the roast on top of the barbecue sauce on the foil and add the other cup of barbecue sauce. Add the potatoes, onions and carrots. Wrap roast tightly and cook on grill turning every 20 minutes for approximately 2 hours.

Teriyaki Steak

4 flank steaks or beef skirt steak
2 cups teriyaki sauce
1/2 teaspoon garlic powder
Large Ziploc® bag

Cut the steak into long strips. In a Ziploc® bag, add the garlic, teriyaki sauce and steak. Let marinate in the refrigerator from 2 hours to overnight, turning occasionally. Preheat grill to medium-hot. Place the steak directly on the grill to cook. Grill about 5 minutes per side.

Brisket Burritos

3 or 4 slices of barbecued beef brisket
1/4 cup onion, chopped
1 tomato, chopped
4 flour tortillas
2 tablespoons oil
1 cup shredded American cheese
1/2 cup salsa

Heat the oil over medium heat in a skillet. Add the brisket slices and cook about 20 minutes until the meat is lightly browned. Cut off any leftover fat, cut the brisket slices into bite size pieces and return the brisket to the skillet. Add the onions and tomatoes and cook for 3 to 5 minutes. Serve on flour tortillas with cheese and salsa.

Campfire Swiss Steak

2 lbs. thick round steak
2 cans tomatoes – 10 oz. cans
1 package of onion soup mix
Salt and pepper to taste

Cut the steak into 3/4" inch pieces. Put the steak in a Dutch oven, add the onion soup on top, salt and pepper, then pour the tomatoes and juice in the Dutch oven. Cover and cook over a low fire for 2 to 3 hours or until meat is tender.

Quick Burritos

1 1/2 pounds lean ground beef
2 cans refried beans, 15 oz. cans
1 teaspoon chili powder
1 teaspoon garlic powder
1 jar of salsa, 16 oz.
Serve with lettuce, shredded cheese, sour cream, flour tortillas

Brown the ground beef and drain. Add a cup of salsa and cook 5 minutes. Add the refried beans, chili powder and garlic powder. Simmer for 15 minutes.

Cowboy Burger

1 1/2 lbs. ground beef
1 package dry onion soup mix
2 teaspoons Worcestershire sauce
1 egg
Salt and pepper to taste
Hamburger buns

Preheat a grill to medium-high heat and spray with Pam®
grilling spray. Combine all ingredients in a bowl. Form into 6
patties. Place the burgers on the grill for 10 to 15 minutes.
Serve with lettuce and tomato.

Charcoal Burgers

1 lb. ground beef
1/8 cup onion, chopped
2 tablespoons water or milk
Salt and pepper to taste
1 can of 10 refrigerated biscuits
1 bottle of barbecue sauce, small
Heavy duty aluminum foil

Mix first 4 ingredients. Form into 4 to 5 patties. Place on large piece of aluminum foil that covers a charcoal grill. Broil 15 to 20 minutes, basting halfway through with barbecue sauce.

Meanwhile, flatten each biscuit to size of hamburger patties. Turn hamburgers and put biscuits on the foil next to them. Bake biscuits about 3 minutes on each side. Serve hamburgers between buttered biscuits with barbecue sauce. Yield: 4 to 5 servings.

Easy Sloppy Joes

1 lb. lean ground beef
1/2 cup onion, chopped
1 can tomato sauce, 8 oz.
1/4 cup ketchup
1 tablespoon apple cider vinegar
1/4 cup packed brown sugar
1 teaspoon Worcestershire sauce
Hamburger buns

Cook the beef and onion in a skillet over medium heat until beef is brown. Drain the fat. Stir in the rest of the ingredients and simmer for 15 to 20 minutes.

Taco Salad

1 lb. ground beef
1 onion, chopped
3 tomatoes, chopped
1/4 cup cilantro, chopped
6 cups lettuce, torn
Crushed tortilla chips
1/2 cup shredded American cheese
Salsa
Pam® cooking spray

Spray Pam® cooking spray in a skillet. Cook the hamburger and onion until beef is no longer pink. Drain the fat. Stir in the tomatoes and cook for a few minutes until tomatoes are tender. Remove from heat and stir in cilantro. Layer the crushed chips on plates with the lettuce on top of chips. Add the meat mixture on top of the lettuce, top off with cheese and salsa.

Dutch Oven Chop Suey

1 lb. cubed pork
1 lb. cubed beef
1 medium onion, chopped
5 stalks celery, chopped
2 cans bean sprouts
1 can Chinese vegetables
2 teaspoons soy sauce
1 tablespoon brown sauce
Salt and pepper

Brown meat in fat in Dutch oven with the celery and onion, add salt and pepper. Drain off some of the fat. Add water to cover meat plus 2 inches over. Cook 2 to 3 hours. Add the cans of bean sprouts and Chinese vegetables (drained).

While that is heating, mix 1/3 cup water, soy sauce and brown sauce. Mix and add to chop suey. Serve over rice.

Spicy Steak Kabobs

1 1/2 lbs. boneless top sirloin steak, thick
1 large bell pepper, cut into large chunks
1 onion, cut into 8 chunks
2 tablespoons chopped cilantro
2 teaspoons hot pepper sauce
2 tablespoons olive oil
1/4 teaspoon garlic powder
1/4 teaspoon red pepper (optional)

Preheat grill to medium-hot. Cut the steak into cubes. Combine the cilantro, pepper sauce, olive oil, garlic powder and red pepper in a medium bowl. Add steak and stir. Thread the beef, onion and bell pepper on six skewers.

Place kabobs over medium-hot coals. Grill about 12 minutes for medium steak, turning occasionally. Yield: 6 servings.

CHICKEN

Quick Chicken Goulash

1 can cream of mushroom soup, 10.5 oz.
1 can green beans, 14.5 oz., drained (save juice)
2 cans chunk chicken breast, 9.75 oz. each
1 large can chow mein noodles, 24 oz.

Stir together the soup, chicken and green beans. If the mixture needs thinning, add some of the green bean juice to thin. Cook until hot and serve over chow mein noodles. Yield: 2 servings.

Grilled Chicken Quesadillas

Tyson Grilled and Ready Chicken Breast Strips (precooked)
1/2 cup shredded Mexican cheese blend
4 flour tortillas
One green onion, chopped
One can of sliced black olives, 2 or 3 oz.
Pam® grilling spray

Combine the cheese, onion and black olives in a small bowl. Cut the cooked chicken breast strips into small bite-size pieces.

Heat grill to medium-high heat. Spray Pam® grilling spray on grill. Put 1 or 2 tortillas on the grill and add a thin layer of chicken and the cheese mixture. Put another tortilla on top and grill about 3 minutes per side. Yield: 2 to 4 servings.

Chicken and Rice

1 can peas, drained (optional)
1 can cream of celery soup, 10.75 oz.
1/2 cup milk
1 can chunk chicken breast, 5 oz.
1 package of Uncle Ben's Ready Rice – Original

Combine the first four ingredients. Heat to boiling. Add package of rice and cook for a few minutes more.

A LITTLE DIRT NEVER HURT

Chicken With Green Chilies

1 can chunk chicken breast, 5 oz.
1 can cream of chicken soup, 10.75 oz.
1 can diced green chilies, 4 oz.
1/3 cup water
1 package of Uncle Ben's Ready Rice – Original or Whole Grain

Combine water and soup. Add green chilies and chicken. Heat and simmer for 10 minutes. Serve over rice.
Serves 2.

Grilled Chicken Fajitas

2 chicken breasts, boneless and skinless
1 bell pepper
1 zucchini
1 yellow squash
1/2 bottle fajita marinade
Flour tortillas
Toppings – cheese, sour cream, salsa
Heavy duty aluminum foil – 2 pieces of 18" x 20"
Large Ziploc® bag

Cut the chicken into 1" pieces. Put the chicken and fajita marinade in a Ziploc® bag and marinate in the refrigerator for 2 hours or overnight, turning occasionally.

Cut the veggies into 1" to 1 1/2" pieces. Spray Pam® on the foil, then add some of the chicken and veggie mixture on each piece of foil. Fold the foil into packets, sealing shut. Repeat making packets until veggies and chicken are gone.

Place packets on a medium-hot grill. Cook for about 20 minutes, turning occasionally until chicken is completely cooked. Serve on flour tortillas with cheese, sour cream and salsa.

Chicken In Foil

4 chicken breasts, boneless and skinless
1 green pepper, chopped
10 mushrooms, chopped
1 can of pineapple slices, 8 oz.
Non-stick cooking spray
Salt and pepper to taste
Heavy duty aluminum foil - 4 pieces of 18" x 20"

Spray the foil with cooking spray. On each of the 4 foils, place an equal amount of mushrooms and peppers. Add a chicken breast on top and a pineapple slice on top of that. Sprinkle with salt and pepper.

Fold the sides of the foil up and seal the edges. Place on a hot grill or coals for 15 minutes, then flip the packets over for another 15 minutes.

Honey Mustard Chicken & Potatoes

4 chicken breasts, boneless and skinless
4 quartered potatoes, cut lengthwise
1 green bell pepper, cut into eight strips
9 tablespoons of honey mustard barbecue sauce
Heavy duty aluminum foil - 4 pieces of 18" x 20"

Place each chicken breast on a piece of foil, add salt and pepper to taste. Add 4 potatoes quarters, 2 strips of green bell pepper and cover with 3 tablespoons of barbecue sauce. Fold the sides of the foil up and seal the edges. Place over hot coals and cook 20 to 25 minutes.

Chicken Hobos

4 chicken breasts, skinless and boneless
1 cup barbecue sauce
1/2 cup chopped green bell pepper
1 can corn, 15.25 oz., drained
Heavy duty aluminum foil

Cut 4 sheets of aluminum foil about 18" each. Place one chicken breast on each sheet of foil. Pour the barbecue sauce over the chicken. Add the bell pepper and corn on top. Fold up the sides of the foil and make a tent, leaving space for heat circulation. Fold the top and ends over making a sealed packet.

Grill about 15 to 20 minutes, covered or until chicken is done.

Teriyaki Chicken Kabobs

1 lb. chicken breasts
Jack Daniel's Teriyaki Marinade
1 red bell pepper
1 green bell pepper
Sliced pineapples, 8 oz., canned
Large Ziploc® bag

Cut the chicken breasts in 1" pieces. Put in Ziploc® bag with the Jack Daniel's marinade. Refrigerate for 4 hours or overnight. Discard marinade.

Cut the bell peppers and sliced pineapples in one inch pieces. Put the chicken, peppers and pineapple on skewers. Grill for about 7 to 8 minutes per side and turn the kabobs every few minutes.

7-Up Barbeque Chicken

4 chicken breasts, bone-in or boneless
1/2 cup soy sauce
1/2 teaspoon horseradish sauce
1 can of regular 7-Up
1/4 cup vegetable oil
Salt to taste
Large Ziploc® bag

Mix all ingredients together in a Ziploc® bag, add the chicken and marinate for 2 hours or overnight in the refrigerator. Grill over medium-high heat.

TURKEY

Ranch Turkey Burgers

1 lb. ground turkey
1/4 cup Worcestershire sauce
1 package ranch dressing mix
1 egg
1/4 cup of bread crumbs (fresh)
1/4 teaspoon garlic powder
Salt and pepper to taste
Hamburger buns
Cheddar cheese slices

Preheat grill with medium high heat, and spray the grill with Pam® for Grilling.

Mix together the ground turkey, ranch dressing, egg, bread crumbs, garlic powder, Worcestershire sauce, salt and pepper in a bowl until well combined. Form into 4 or 5 patties. Grill the patties about 5 minutes on each side. (165 degrees F with a meat thermometer). Add one slice of cheddar cheese on each patty the last minute. Serve on buns with lettuce, tomato and red onion.

Note: If the burgers seem too moist to place right on the grill, try grilling for about 3 minutes on each side on aluminum foil (sprayed with Pam®) on the grill, then remove the aluminum foil and place the burgers directly on the grill.

Just Another Turkey Burger

1 pound ground turkey breast
Hamburger buns
1 egg
1/4 cup dry bread crumbs
1 teaspoon brown mustard
1/4 teaspoon black pepper
1/4 teaspoon thyme

Combine the last 5 ingredients in a bowl. Add the turkey and mix. Shape mixture into 4 patties. Grill for 8 to 10 minutes on each side or until turkey is done. Serve on buns.

PORK

Sausage with Barbecue Beans

1 can barbecue beans, 16 oz.
6 to 8 sausage links
1/2 green pepper, chopped
1/2 onion, chopped
Shredded American cheese

Cook the sausage until they are browned. Drain the sausage fat, leaving just a little and cook the onion and green pepper in the fat until tender. Add the beans and heat for 10 minutes. Top with cheese when finished.

Easy Peasy Sausage and Potatoes

1/2 pound bulk pork sausage
1 large onion
2 large potatoes

Crumble the sausage into a frying pan. Dice the potatoes and onion. Add the potatoes and onion to the sausage and cook over low heat until the potatoes are tender and sausage is cooked. Drain fat. Yield: 2 servings.

Campfire Sausage-Veggie Dinner

1 lb. Polish sausage
3 medium baking potatoes
1 bell pepper, cut into strips
3 carrots, cut into 3 x 1/2" strips
1 medium onion, sliced
1 cup water

Cut the sausage diagonally into 1/2 inch slices. Wash potatoes, leaving skin on. Cut potatoes into 1/4" slices. Layer in order - the potatoes, sausage, bell pepper, carrots and onion in a Dutch oven. Sprinkle with salt and pepper. Add water, bring to a boil. Cover and reduce heat. Simmer for about 45 minutes or until vegetables are tender.

Ham and Green Beans

1 cup ham, diced
1 can green beans, 15.25 oz., drained
1/3 cup mayonnaise
1 package of Uncle Ben's Ready Rice
1 1/3 cups chicken bouillon
1 small package parmesan cheese
Heavy duty aluminum foil – 18" x 24", doubled over

Combine first 5 ingredients in a bowl. Sprinkle with Parmesan
cheese. Shape the doubled over foil into a bowl. Put the
mixture in the aluminum foil bowl and seal the foil. Place on
hot coals for about 30 minutes.

Barbecued Pork Chops

Center cut pork chops (1" thick)
McCormick Grill Mates® Montreal Steak Seasoning
Heavy duty aluminum foil

Sprinkle the pork chops generously on both sides with the seasoning. Grill over coals, turning frequently until pork chops are brown on both sides. Then wrap in heavy duty aluminum foil, adding 2 to 3 tablespoons of water; steam on the back of the grill about 30 minutes or until pork chops are done.

Hobo Sausage Dinner

1 lb. smoked sausage
2 onions
2 cans green beans, 15.25 oz.
1/2 lb. red potatoes, quartered
Salt and pepper to taste
1 packet of Zesty Italian seasoning
1 teaspoon vegetable oil
1 teaspoon margarine
1/4 cup water
Pam® cooking spray
Heavy duty aluminum foil – 18" x 24"

Preheat a grill on high heat. Spray the foil with Pam®. Cut the sausage into 1" pieces. Slice the onions.

Place the sausage, potatoes, green beans and onion on the aluminum foil. Season with salt and pepper, sprinkle with the Italian seasoning and oil, then add the margarine on the top. Gather up the sides of the foil, and then pour the water in the packet. Fold the edges over and seal tightly to form a packet. Grill for 30 to 40 minutes, turning at least once. Sausage should be browned and veggies tender, when done.

BBQ Spareribs

2 to 3 pounds pork spareribs
Barbecue sauce
Salt and pepper

Salt and pepper the ribs. Grill ribs, covered, over medium hot coals and indirect heat. Grill until the ribs are tender, 1 1/2 to 2 hours. Turn occasionally and baste with barbecue sauce. Add more charcoal halfway through, if necessary, to keep the grill temperature at about 325 to 350 F.

 TAKE A HIKE

Sausage in Foil

1 lb. fully cooked Polish sausage, sliced in 1/2" pieces
1 onion, sliced
1 green pepper
4 carrots, sliced in 1/4" pieces
4 potatoes, sliced in 1/2" pieces
1 cabbage, sliced
2 chopped tomatoes
Margarine
Salt and pepper to taste
Heavy duty aluminum foil – 4 pieces 18" x 24"

Spray foil with non-stick cooking spray. Place 1/4 of the sausage in the center of each foil. Add the sliced onions on top of the sausage. Add the green pepper on top, then the rest of the vegetables. Salt and pepper the veggies. Dot with margarine.

Fold the sides of the foil up as if making a tent. Take the top edges and fold them over together. Then on each end, bring together and fold the edges over together. Be sure the foil is sealed tightly. It will cook faster if it is air tight. Cook over coals 30 minutes depending on the coals until the vegetables are tender.

Yield: 4 servings.

FISH

Beer Fish

Fish fillets
Vegetable oil
Potato chips
1 can of beer

Pour beer into a large bowl, then place fillets into bowl and let them soak for about 10 minutes. Crush chips and set aside. Heat vegetable oil in a cast iron skillet until hot. Coat the fish with crushed chips and deep fry in skillet until golden brown, approximately 15 minutes.

Grilled Fish

4 fish fillets
1 onion, sliced
1 tomato, sliced
1 lemon, sliced
Heavy duty aluminum foil – 4 pieces of 18' x 20"
Pam® cooking spray
Salt and pepper

Generously spray Pam® on each foil. Place a fish on each foil; salt and pepper the fish. On each fish, layer the onion slices, tomato slices, and lemon slices. Seal the foil tightly and place on a preheated grill. When the aluminum foil inflates from the steam, poke a small hole in the foil. Cook for 20 to 30 minutes.

Quick Tuna Lunch

2 cans of tuna, 5 oz.
1/3 cup of milk
1 teaspoon dry minced onion
Bag of potato chips
Combine first 3 ingredients in a saucepan. Heat the mixture until bubbly, stirring often. Serve the mixture over potato chips.

Serves 2.

 **DID YOU HEAR THAT!**

Tuna Surprise

1 can tuna, 5 oz.
2 tablespoons margarine
2 tablespoons flour
1 can tomatoes, 14.5 oz. drained
1/2 teaspoon yellow mustard
1 egg, slightly beaten
1 cup grated American cheese
1/2 teaspoon Worcestershire source
1 small onion, chopped fine
Salt to taste

Melt butter and add seasonings, tomatoes, flour, cheese and egg. Cook for just a few minutes. Heat milk to scalding point and add to other ingredients. Then add can of tuna. Let simmer for five minutes. Serve over rice or noodles or on toast.

Lemon Pepper Salmon

4 salmon fillets
2 teaspoons dill weed
2 teaspoons chili powder
1 teaspoon lemon pepper seasoning
Salt and pepper
Pam® grilling spray

Combine the dill weed, chili powder and lemon pepper seasoning in a small bowl. Rub on each salmon filet. Preheat grill to medium-hot heat and spray with Pam®. Grill the fish with the skin side down for about 20 minutes or until fish flakes easily with a fork.

SIDES

Easy Smoked Veggies

1 can of French-style green beans, 15.25 oz.
1 can of sliced or whole potatoes
Margarine
Mesquite wood chips
Heavy duty aluminum foil

Grilling - Put the wood chips down first and then put the coals on top.

Make a foil pouch, drain the canned vegetables, pour them into the foil, throw butter on top, close the pouch and put on grill. Cook until heated through.

Grilled Tomatoes

2 large tomatoes
1 tablespoon packaged ranch dressing mix
Parmesan cheese or another shredded white cheese
Pam® cooking spray

Cut the tomatoes in half. Spray Pam® in a frying pan. Put the tomatoes cut side up in the frying pan. Sprinkle the Ranch salad dressing on each tomato. Add the cheese on top. Cover and cook until tomatoes are heated through.

Tomato Zucchini

1 lb. zucchini, sliced
2 cans of diced tomatoes with Basil or Italian Seasonings,
14.5 oz.
Salt and pepper to taste

Combine sliced zucchini, tomatoes, salt and pepper in pan
and cook for about 20 minutes or until zucchini is cooked.

 SINGIN' ROUND THE CAMPFIRE

Campfire Mac and Cheese

1 box Kraft Deluxe Macaroni and Cheese
1 can tuna, 5 oz., drained
1 can of Italian breadcrumbs

Add macaroni to boiling water. Cook until tender. Add the pack of cheese and the can of drained tuna. Transfer to plates and sprinkle the breadcrumbs on top.

Potatoes in Foil

1 potato per person
Margarine
Salt and pepper to taste
(add sliced onion if desired)

Clean the potatoes and slice them into thick slices, leaving the peeling on. Place each potato in heavy duty aluminum foil. Add a tablespoon of margarine and sprinkle with salt and pepper. Seal the foil tightly and cook, grill for about 1 hour. Turn the potato packages often.

Corn in Foil

2 ears of corn
Margarine
Salt and pepper
Aluminum foil

Remove all the husks except the last layer. Also remove the silk. Pull the remaining husks back and spread the margarine on the corn. Add salt and pepper.

Pull the husks back over the corn and tightly wrap them with foil. Place on hot coals for 15 minutes then turn and cook for 15 more minutes. Yield: 2 servings.

Sweet Onion Blossom

1 large sweet onion
1 1/2 teaspoon margarine
Salt and pepper
Aluminum foil

Preheat grill on high. Peel an onion and make 6 to 8 cuts down to the base (leave base intact). Gently pull the onion wedges apart a bit. Put the butter, salt and pepper inside the onion.

Wrap onion very tightly with foil and place on grill. Cooking time is approximately 45 minutes. Onion should be lightly brown and translucent.

Easy Chili

1 can of chili with beans, 15 oz.
1 can tomato soup, 10.75 oz.
1 can bean with bacon soup, 11.5 oz.
1 1/2 cups water

Combine all ingredients and simmer for 15 minutes.

 **GETTING BACK TO NATURE**

Campground Chili

1 cup lentils
1 tablespoon cumin
3 tablespoons tomato soup powder
1 teaspoon oregano
1 clove garlic
1 tablespoon chili powder
1 tablespoon onion flakes
Salt and pepper
4 cups water

Combine all the ingredients and simmer 30 to 45 minutes.

Grilled Mushrooms

1/2 pound whole mushrooms
1/4 cup butter
1/2 teaspoon garlic salt

Place the mushrooms on skewers. Melt the butter and add the garlic salt. Grill mushrooms over medium-high heat for 10 to 15 minutes, brushing with the butter and salt mixture and turning periodically.

Camper's Baked Potatoes

2 baking potatoes
1 onion
2 tablespoons margarine
Salt and pepper to taste
Non-stick cooking spray
Heavy duty aluminum foil – 2 pieces 18" x 18"

Preheat grill on medium-hot heat. Slice the potatoes leaving the peeling on. Slice the onion. Spray the foil with non-stick cooking spray. On the center of a large sheet of foil, place half of the potatoes and onion. Add salt and pepper and 1 tablespoon margarine. Repeat for the other half of the potatoes and onion.

Gather up the edges of the aluminum foil making a packet, and seal the edges. Place the packet on the grill and cook for about 30 minutes turning occasionally.

Grilled Garlic Bread

1 French bread loaf
1 teaspoon garlic powder
1/4 cup margarine
Heavy duty aluminum foil

Preheat grill on medium heat. Cut the bread into thick slices. Spread the margarine on both sides of each slice of bread. Sprinkle lightly with garlic powder. Reassemble the loaf and wrap in foil, sealing tightly. Grill for 15 to 20 minutes, turning once.

Poor Man's Beans

1 can pork & beans, 28 oz.
2 cans Vienna sausage, 4 oz. cans
1/3 cup ketchup
1/2 teaspoon prepared mustard
Hamburger buns

Combine first 4 ingredients in a skillet and heat until boiling. Spoon generous helpings on hamburger buns. Serve with pickles.

FIRE UP THE GRILL!

Roasted Corn

2 ears of corn
1/4 cup mayonnaise
1/4 teaspoon garlic powder
1/4 teaspoon paprika
1/4 teaspoon parsley flakes
Salt and pepper
Heavy duty aluminum foil

Preheat grill to medium heat. Combine the mayonnaise, garlic powder, paprika, parsley flakes, salt and pepper in a bowl. Remove the husks and silk from the ears of corn. Spread the mayonnaise mixture over corn. Wrap each ear of corn separately in foil. Grill, covered, for 30 to 40 minutes or until corn is tender.

Skillet Baked Beans

2 cans of pork and beans (16 to 18 oz.)
3/4 cup brown sugar
1 teaspoon dry mustard
1/2 cup ketchup
6 slices of fully cooked bacon, crumbled
Pam® cooking spray

Spray Pam® in a large skillet. Add 1 can of the pork and beans. Mix the brown sugar, dry mustard, crumbled bacon and ketchup together in a bowl. Place the mixture over the pork and beans in the skillet. Add the other can of beans on top. Cook on low heat for 30 minutes or more, stirring occasionally.

Sautéed Zucchini

2 small zucchini
2 tablespoons of margarine
Salt and pepper

With a sharp knife, cut each zucchini crosswise into thirds, then cut each into eight wedges. Over medium heat, melt margarine in a small skillet. When margarine is very hot, add zucchini, salt and pepper. Cook, stirring constantly, until tender crisp, about 5 minutes.

Grilled Sweet Potatoes

1 large sweet potato
1 tablespoon margarine
Salt and pepper
Heavy duty aluminum foil – 18" x 18"
Pam® cooking spray

Preheat grill to medium-high heat. Cut the potato in half lengthwise. Spray the foil with Pam®. Place a potato half in the center of the foil. Spread the cut side of the potato with butter, salt and pepper. Place the other half of the potato on top of this half.

Gather the foil around the potato, sealing tightly. Grill, covered, over medium-hot heat for 30 minutes or until potato is done, turning a couple times.

Italian Green Beans

1/2 pound fresh green beans
2 tablespoons zesty Italian salad dressing
1/2 teaspoon salt

In a Dutch oven, bring 2 quarts water with salt to a boil. (Covering the Dutch oven with a lid or aluminum foil will allow the water to boil.) Cut the beans into one inch pieces.

After the water is boiling, add the beans and reduce heat to medium. Cook for 5 minutes or until tender. Drain water and put the beans in a bowl. Add salad dressing and toss to coat.

Biscuit Twisters

Refrigerated bread stick dough
Honey or jelly

Unwrap each bread stick and roll it between your palms. Then twist the dough around the end of a stick (soak stick in water first so it doesn't burn). Hold the stick over hot coals until cooked, rotating constantly. Dip into honey or spread with jelly.

 **COZY CAMPFIRE**

PIZZA

French Bread Pizza

1 lb. hamburger (or use a package of turkey pepperoni)
1/2 cup onion, chopped
1 jar pizza sauce, 14 oz.
1 can sliced ripe olives, 2 or 3 oz.
1 cup shredded Mozzarella cheese
1 loaf of French bread
Heavy duty aluminum foil

Brown the hamburger and onion. Drain. Stir in the jar of pizza sauce and cook for 10 minutes. Cut the French bread in 4 pieces – cut in half lengthwise and then widthwise. Spread the sauce and meat on each piece of bread. Add the olives and cheese on top of the sauce.

Wrap each piece of bread separately in heavy duty aluminum foil. Be sure the foil is sealed well. Grill for 15 to 20 minutes covered or cook over coals until pizza is done.

Mini Pizzas

1 can refrigerator biscuits
2 cups mozzarella cheese, shredded
1 cup pizza sauce
Pepperoni and other toppings as desired
Heavy duty aluminum foil
Pam® cooking spray

Preheat grill to medium-high heat. Roll each biscuit into a 6 inch round piece of dough. Spray a 12" piece of aluminum foil with Pam® cooking spray. One sheet will hold 2 mini-pizzas. Place 2 of the pizza dough in the center of the foil, leaving 3" at the top and bottom of the foil. Bend the excess foil up so you can grab the foil by the edge "handles".

Place on grill and cook covered for about 2 to 5 minutes. Watch carefully. When the bottom is lightly browned, remove the dough from the grill by the foil handles. Flip each mini pizza over, and put back on the grill for about another 2 minutes or so. Remove from grill and add pizza sauce and toppings. Place back on the grill and cook, covered, for 3 to 8 minutes.

Dutch Oven Pizza

1 can refrigerated pizza dough
1 cup pizza sauce
1 package sliced pepperoni
8 oz. package of shredded mozzarella cheese
Disposable aluminum foil pie plate
Pam® cooking spray

Spray the pie plate lightly with Pam®. Spread the pizza dough on the bottom and up the sides of the pie tin. Add the pizza sauce, pepperoni and cheese.

Place 4 small rocks or balls of aluminum foil in a Dutch oven so the pizza isn't sitting right on the bottom of the Dutch oven. Put the pizza in the Dutch oven and cook for 10 to 15 minutes. Note: Put more heat on the top (more briquettes) of the Dutch oven than the bottom.

Pizza on the Grill

Refrigerated pizza dough
1 jar pizza sauce, 14 oz.
Olive oil
8 oz. package shredded mozzarella cheese
Turkey pepperoni
Other toppings as desired
Pam® for grilling

Preheat the grill on high. Spray the grill with Pam®. Unroll the refrigerated pizza dough and separate into 2 sections. This makes 2 pizzas. Use one section for each pizza. Shape the pizza dough and flatten the entire piece of dough. (Don't build the dough up around the edges).

Once the grill is hot, place the pizza dough on a greased large plate or cookie sheet and slide it off the plate onto the grill. Grill, covered, for 2 minutes. Check after 2 minutes and if the dough is not starting to brown, cook for another minute and check again. Repeat until the dough is light brown. Be very careful not to burn the crust. Remove from grill.

Use a small amount of olive oil on the pizza dough. Then add some pizza sauce and the rest of the toppings. (Don't weigh the pizza down with too many toppings) Reduce the heat of the grill and put the pizza back on the grill. Grill, covered, 2 to 3 minutes longer or until cheese is melted.

HOT DOGS

Favorite Chili Dogs

4 hot dogs
4 hot dog buns
1 can hot dog chili, 15 oz.
1/4 cup onions
1/2 cup shredded cheddar cheese
Pam® cooking spray
Aluminum foil

Put a hot dog in each bun. Top each with 1/4 can of chili, 2 tablespoons shredded cheese and onion. Lightly spray the cheese with cooking spray. Wrap each hot dog separately in aluminum foil and place over fire for 20 minutes or until cheese has melted completely.

Cheesy Hot Dogs on a Stick

8 hot dogs
8 slices of bacon
Cheddar cheese, sliced
Toothpicks

Split the hot dog lengthwise almost to the end. Place cheese strips inside the spilt hot dog. Wrap the hot dog with bacon and secure with a toothpick. Roast over an open fire until the bacon becomes crispy and the hot dog is well heated.

Hobo Hot Dogs in Foil

4 hot dogs
4 hot dog buns
1 onion, chopped
4 tablespoons pickle relish
4 oz. shredded American cheese
Heavy duty aluminum foil – 4 pieces 18" x 18"

Put each hot dog in a hot dog bun. Top with chopped onion, shredded cheese and pickle relish. Wrap each hot dog separately in aluminum foil and place over fire for 20 minutes or until cheese has melted completely.

Beanie Wienies

1 can of baked beans
2 hot dogs
2 hot dog buns
1/2 cup barbecue sauce
Heavy duty aluminum foil - 2 pieces 18" x 18"

Place each hot dog on a separate piece of aluminum foil. Spread barbecue sauce on each hot dog. Add baked beans on top of hot dogs. Wrap tightly and place on hot coals. When heated, place the contents of the aluminum foil on a hot dog bun.

Butterfly Hot Dogs

1 package of hot dogs
1 package of hot dog buns
1/2 cup barbecue sauce

Slit hot dogs length-wise, being careful not to cut all the way through. Open flat; brush the cut side with barbecue sauce and grill, turning once. Serve in hot dog buns or on a mound of baked beans.

FIRE UP THE GRILL!

No Fail Hot Dogs

1 package of hot dogs
Refrigerated breadstick dough
Sticks or skewers

Put the hot dogs on the sticks or skewers. Separate the breadstick dough and roll between palms into a 4 or 5" strip. Wind breadstick dough around hot dog. Pinch tightly at each end to hold. Toast over coals turning slowly to cook through and brown evenly, about 5 minutes.

Quick Dog Kabobs

1 package of hot dogs
Large stuffed green olives
1 can pineapple chunks, 20 oz. (or fresh)
1 package of fully cooked bacon
1/8 cup soy sauce
1/8 cup vegetable oil

Cut each hot dog into 5 pieces. Thread on skewers along with the olives and pineapple chunks wrapped in half slices of bacon. Brush with mixture of half soy sauce and half salad oil. Cook until the bacon is crispy.

DESSERTS

Campfire Apples

1 apple
1 apple
1 tablespoon brown sugar
1/4 teaspoon cinnamon

Mix the brown sugar and cinnamon in a bowl. Core the apple. Spoon the mixture into the center. Wrap the apple in aluminum foil. Place on hot coals for 15 to 20 minutes per side.

Baked Bananas

6 firm bananas
1/2 cup brown sugar
1/2 teaspoon cinnamon
Skewers

With the peeling on the bananas, cut the bananas in 1 inch slices. Mix the brown sugar and cinnamon together. Dip each cut end of the bananas in the brown sugar mixture. Thread the bananas on skewers.

Hold over coals until hot and the banana peel turns brown. Dip the bananas in the remaining brown sugar mixture to eat.

Dutch Oven Spice Cake

1 box spice cake mix
2 cans of apple pie filling, 16 oz. cans
1 can of root beer, 12 oz.
2 tablespoons butter
12 quart Dutch oven

Preheat the Dutch oven on medium-hot heat. Melt the butter in the pan. Put the pie filling on top of the melted butter and sprinkle the cake mix evenly over the fruit. Pour in a can of root beer.

Cover the Dutch oven with lid. Put 10 charcoal briquettes on the bottom of the Dutch oven and 18 on top. Cook for 50 minutes to 1 hour or until cake turns a golden brown.

Grilled Peaches

4 large peaches
2 teaspoons honey
Pam® grilling spray and cooking spray

Cut the peaches in half, remove the peach pits. Set the peaches so the cut side is up and lightly spray cut side with Pam® cooking spray.

Preheat the grill to medium heat. Spray the grill with Pam® grilling spray. Put the peaches on the grill, cut side down and cook about 2 minutes until the skin splits. Flip the peaches and cook for about 2 more minutes. Remove from grill and drizzle each peach with 1/4 teaspoon of honey.

Cinnamon Apples

1/4 cup red cinnamon candies
4 teaspoons brown sugar
4 tart apples – cored
Heavy duty aluminum foil – 4 pieces 18" x 12" each

Place one cored apple in center of a 12 inch piece of foil. Fill the center with 1 tablespoon of red cinnamon candies and 1 teaspoon brown sugar. Fold the foil tightly over the apple and seal well. Grill over medium hot heat for 30 minutes or until apples are tender.

Honey Biscuit Treats

1 can refrigerated biscuits
Honey or jam

Pull or cut each biscuit in half. Using your palms, roll the half biscuit until you have an elongated piece of dough. Place it on the end of a skewer or stick that has been soaked in water. Toast the dough over the fire about 10 minutes or until the dough is cooked. Fill it with honey or jam.

Chocolate Bananas

1 banana
1/2 chocolate bar or chocolate chips
1 package mini-marshmallows
Heavy duty aluminum foil

Make a cut in the banana from one end to the other leaving the banana peel on. Pry the banana open a little and insert chocolate and marshmallows. If using a chocolate bar, break it into tiny pieces. Wrap the banana in foil and place on a grill or hot coals. Cook for 10 minutes or until chocolate is melted.

Dutch Oven Dump Cake

1 can cherry pie filling, 21 oz.
1 can crushed pineapple, 15 oz.
1 package yellow cake mix
1/2 cup butter
12" Dutch oven

"Dump" the cherry pie filling and pineapple in a Dutch oven and mix. Sprinkle the cake mix evenly and smoothly on top of the fruit mixture. Add pieces of butter on top. Place 15 coals on top of the Dutch oven and 13 coals under the Dutch oven. Cook for about 40 minutes or until golden brown. Rotate the pan occasionally.

S'mores

4 Hershey bars
1 package graham crackers
1 package large marshmallows
Coat hangers or skewers

Break one graham cracker in half. Cover one of the graham crackers with part of a Hershey bar. Roast 2 marshmallows on a skewer over the fire until soft. Then place the marshmallows on top of the Hershey bar and cover with the other graham cracker.

Apples in Foil

4 apples, peeled and cored
1/2 cup nuts
1/2 cup shredded coconut
1/2 cup raisins
1 cup brown sugar

Be careful not to cut through one end of the apple when coring. After peeling and coring the apples, place them on separate pieces of heavy duty aluminum foil. Fill the apple centers (the hole) with nuts, coconut and raisins. Sprinkle generously with brown sugar. Fold the foil around each apple tightly. Place in coals and cook for 20 to 40 minutes. Yield: 4 servings.

MISCELLANEOUS

Campfire Popcorn

2 tablespoons oil
2 tablespoon popcorn kernels
Heavy duty aluminum foil
Butter, melted
Salt

Use an 18" length of foil and put the oil and popcorn in the center. Gather the corners of the foil together, making a loose pouch with lots of room for expansion, sealing well. Tie the foil packet to a long stick with string. Place the pouch over hot coals, shaking continually until all the popcorn pops. Add butter and salt when finished.

Frito Pie

Fritos
Lettuce – chopped
Cheddar cheese, shredded
1 can of chili without beans, 15 oz.
1/2 onion, diced

Heat the chili. Arrange fritos on a plate. Add the chili on top of the fritos. Add the lettuce, cheese and onions.

Chili-Cheese Dip

1 can chili without beans, 15 oz.
1/2 cup sharp cheese, shredded

Heat the chili. Let stand at back of grill 10 to 15 minutes until some of liquid has evaporated. Blend in the cheese. Stir until cheese is melted. Use as dip for chips, veggies or use corn or flour tortillas to dip.

A-HIKING WE WILL GO!

Sun Tea

4 Family size tea bags
1 gallon of water

Use a glass gallon container with a screw-on lid. (The screw-on lid is to keep ants out.) Fill with water and add the 4 tea bags. Let the container sit in the sun for about 6 hours. Serve with lemon and sugar.

Camper's Coffee

3/4 cup sugar
1 cup powdered non-dairy creamer
3/4 cup instant coffee
3/4 cup instant hot chocolate
1/4 teaspoon ground nutmeg
1/2 teaspoon ground cinnamon

Mix all ingredients together and put in sealed jar. This would be best to make at home before camping. Use 3 teaspoons of the coffee mixture with 1 cup of hot water, more or less to taste.

Other Books by Bonnie Scott

Grill It!
100 Easy Recipes in Jars
Soups, Sandwiches and Wraps

Slow Cooker Comfort Foods
Fish & Game Cookbook

All titles available in Paperback and Kindle versions at Amazon.com

DIY Camping Projects

www.CampingFreebies.com

Made in the USA
Lexington, KY
01 July 2013